Viable

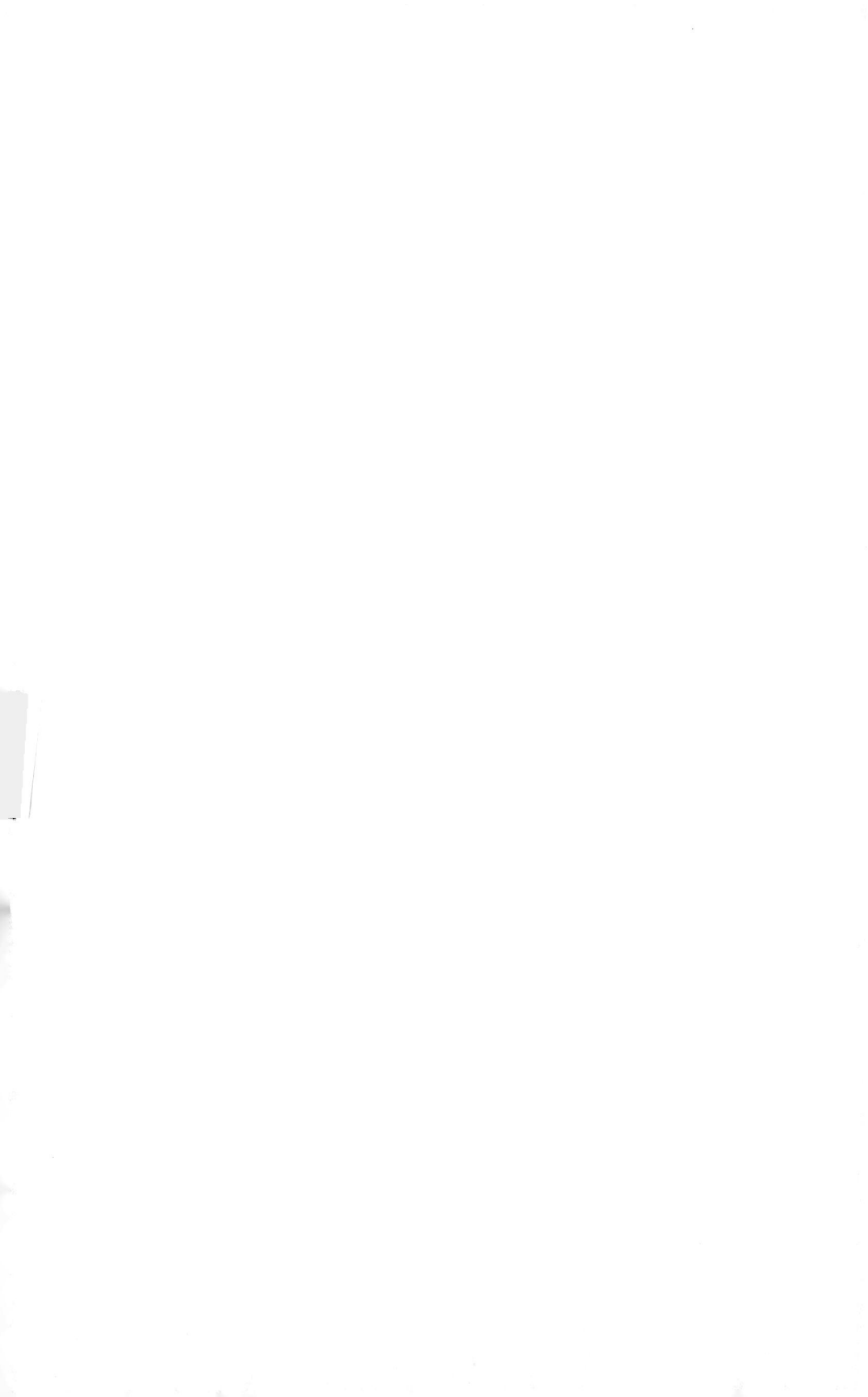

Viable

Julie Hensley

Five Oaks Press
FIVE-OAKS-PRESS.COM

Copyright © Julie Hensley
All rights reserved. First edition

Five Oaks Press
Newburgh, NY 12550
five-oaks-press.com
editor@five-oaks-press.com

ISBN: 978-0-9907842-7-2

Cover Art: Footage Firm

Author photo: John R. McQuiston

Printed in the United States of America

Acknowledgements

Grateful acknowledgement is made to the editors of the following publications, where some of the poems in this book first appeared:

4ink7, "Little Deaths," "These Terrible Times," "Blackwork Solstice," "The Work of Women," "Even Stones Come to Rest"

Gulf Stream Literary Review, "For Her to Enter This World"

Saranac Review, "Dark Moon," "Divination," and "That Kind of Fortune"

Ruminate, "Winter Without," "My Mother with Horses" *

Becoming Woman, "Kerosene" *

Alligator Juniper, "Returning to Water" * and "Still Life of Aunt Alice" *

Southern Women's Review, "Viable" and "Moving Water"

PoemMemoirStory, "Pica"

Superstition Review, "Bajada" *

Cadence of Hooves: A Celebration of Horses, "Blessing, North of Perigoux" *

Sea, Sand, Sail, "In the Outer Banks" *

Karamu, "Rise" *

Blueline, "Winter and Homesick" *

Briar Cliff Review, "Thinking of My Mother, Twenty-eight Years, Six Months" *

Petroglyph, "Kerosene" (as "A Summer") *

Louisiana Literature, "Unknowns" *

The Language of Horses, Finishing Line Press, 2011, "French Braiding," "Shadow Story," "Resurrections," "The Language of Horses," "Mapping the Air," "Mother's Wishes," and "Monsoon Season," (in addition to poems marked with an asterisk above).

Many thanks to Five Oaks Editor Lynn Houston, whose wisdom transformed my manuscript into a beautiful book. This project was also generously supported by Kentucky Arts Council, Kentucky Foundation for Women, and Hambidge Center for the Creative Arts and Sciences.

Thanks to the teachers and professors with whom I've had the privilege of studying poetry throughout the years: Jeff Newton, Edward Huffstetler, Pinkie Gordon Lane, Elizabeth Dodd, Jonathan Holden, and Alberto Rios. Also integral to my education were a handful of brilliant poet friends and colleagues who provided immeasurable mentorship, inspiration, and support: John Olivares Espinoza, Miles Waggener, John Morris, Margaret Frozena, Harry Brown, Dorothy Sutton, Libby Falk Jones, Christina Lovin, Young Smith, and Becky Blanton McGee. They read early versions of these poems, helped me navigate publishing, and infused the often-solitary poet's world with warmth and fun.

Thanks to my family: Nana Bobbie, the first published poet I ever met; my father, Mike Hensley, the scientist who can quote Robert Frost from memory; my sisters, the girls who once convinced me I was adopted (Why else did I have such frizzy, blonde hair? Why was I the only one afraid of horses?) yet somehow never teased me about *this*. For this book, in particular, I'm indebted to my mother, Joy Hensley, who in encouraging my early reading and writing, conceived so much of what sustains me now. More importantly, she mothered me with love and grace and humor, ensuring that *Viable* was a book I would eventually have to write.

I'm grateful to the midwives Ann Stewart and Jamie Atwood who shepherded my children into this world: the first was willing to wait more than two days, and the second was willing to let a pizza burn in the oven when it was clear there would be no waiting. I have no doubt that the births these women helped me achieve shaped my feelings about motherhood as a source of empowerment and a wellspring of creativity. I'm indebted also to Deb Core who, with a small gesture, spurred my spiritual journey at a much needed time.

And, as always, the greatest thanks goes to Bob Johnson, my partner in all endeavors, and to my children—equal parts inspiritirs and saboteurs, Boyd and Maeve keep my creative life balanced.

Contents

That Kind of Fortune   5

Fingerprint
My Mother with Horses   8
French Braiding   10
Returning to Water   11
Kerosene   12
Shadow Story   13
Unknowns   14
Resurrections   16
The Language of Horses   18
Mapping the Air   21
Mother's Wishes   22
In the Outer Banks   23
Winter and Homesick   24
Rise   25
Monsoon Season   26
A Fingerprint, Carried Long and Quiet   28
Blessing, North of Perigueux   29

I, Who Finally Dissolved
Little Deaths   32
At My Desk, Ten Weeks Pregnant   34
Thinking of My Mother, 28 Years and Six Months   35
Pica   36
Dry Leaves   37
Divination   38
Dark Moon   40

Winter Without
Blackwork Solstice   44
Viable   46
Phantom   49
After the First Miscarriage   50
Bunraku   51

Conflagration   53
Proof   55
After the Second Miscarriage   58
Winter Without   59
Bajada   60

For Her to Enter This World
These Terrible Times   64
Prayer from Cedar Creek Falls   67
For Her to Enter This World   68
Moving Water   70

Your Pulse
The Work of Women   74
A Large Body of Water   77
We Had Been Promised   79
Still Life of Aunt Alice   82
Gloria   83

My Own Skin
Even Stones Come to Rest   86
Space   89
Ordinary Time   91
Show and Tell, or Family Math   95
Fever-Cord   98
What Boyd Knows   99
My Own Skin   100
Biohazard   102

For Boyd and Maeve, always my greatest works.
And for Gus and Ann.

That Kind of Fortune
    for Bob

We slept apart that June,
though we were still new
to our wedding bed. You,
in a writers' studio, surrounded
by the din of tree frogs, I,
in the loft of a cedar-sided garden cottage,
ten miles of gravel road twisting
between us. There were days of rain
when fog rising off the creeks
made the distance more tangible.

We were trying to finish
our first books, trying to decide
if we were ready to have a child.
Without you, my skin rebelled—
the little hairs on my arms rose
every time I cracked the window.
Through filmy glass, the world,
ever-damp, nudged toward sunlight
in pale green stalks of asparagus,
in tendrils of sugar-snap peas,
their creamy blossoms shivering.
Above me, even the roof shingles
sprouted moss like sleek fur.

I had to cross moving water
to reach you, had to pedal past
a den of red foxes, little more, at first,
than nose-quiver and eye-shine,
but soon the kits tumbled in the brush,
stretched their coppery backs and yawned
long into any sun-soaked moment.
I was always sweat-slicked,
legs shaking, by the time I dismounted
to push the bike up the final ridge.

A decade before, when I found myself
in a nearby desk, I watched you
bend and scratch something into a notebook,
liking the way your left elbow lifted
to protect your words, liking the careful
curve I knew your hands must have pressed
into the bill of your Reds cap. Did you know I slid
you inside my pocket that afternoon?
Ready to warm you against my thigh
for as many years as it might take.
Like the arrowhead I once lifted
from the tall grass along the gas line—when you looked up,
your smile marked that kind of fortune.

I found a sign woven into a nest wrens had made
beneath the eaves of my cottage—a snake skin
braided through twigs and mud, one long piece
draped so the breeze could lift it like a flag,
thin as onion peel, mottled where the scales had
shed the burden of the previous season. I thought
of the bird, how she must have hesitated,
hung in the air for a moment, before swooping
to retrieve such dangerous treasure.

Fingerprint

My Mother with Horses

It started in Big Stone Gap in the front yard
where my sisters and I fashioned whatever we could find—
tricycles, broom handles, a leaf rake—into a kind of dressage course.
She lay with a book by our plastic pool,
shaded her eyes and watched us weave through on stick ponies,
clicking our tongues, avoiding the holes
the dog dug by the porch and along the wrought iron fence.

We rode the school bus to the public library where she worked,
where there was Misty of Chincoteague, The Red Pony, and Billy and Blaze.
If she was busy or we were loud,
she would sit us in the back on the blue carpet
to watch filmstrips about Pony Penning Day.

She wanted those two pinto ponies, lesson animals
who nickered when we leaned out the car windows,
who licked sugar from our palms.
For years afterwards she thought she saw them down dirt roads,
ordered my father to have a look
on the way home from Sandbridge or Buckrow Beach.
Finally a Welsh saddle pony—
old and nearly unrideable—was the first we could afford.
There is a picture of her in my father's drawer, hair wild,
hips small in brown corduroys, holding the halter
as my youngest sister and I lean off an abandoned hay wagon
to caress the brown fur.

I was still young when she found the Arabian Quarter horse mix,
a mare who had miscarried many times.
That winter I held the cord of a sled that would not move
across the half inch of frozen snow.
I sat next to my sister—both of us stiff in snow suits—
watched her drag cinder blocks
and a rotting fence post from behind the barn,
watched them rise together,

the horse's tail spreading like light against the gray sky.

This is how she washed our hair:
She pulled a wicker bottomed chair to the kitchen sink
leaned into our backs, one at a time,
lathered and rinsed Prell from a green bottle,
then held each of us, squirming, between her knees
and worked out the snarls with a wide-toothed comb.

She awaits the first birth in a house without daughters,
a foal swelling and turning inside
the brood mare she gave her only girl grandchild.
I imagine she takes her time now,
moving the curry comb in slow circles,
letting the winter dander float
like milkweed from her fingers.

French Braiding

In our room was a doll with a blond flip,
just a head, really, and a neck, pale and rubbery,
anchored in a six palette eye shadow base,
planted like the ferns drying on our mother's porch.

There was a drawer beneath the bathroom counter
where tools rattled in a colorful tangle:
plastic combs, yellowing brushes, ribbons and rubber bands
whose knotted centers and brass clasps sprouted
tufts of shimmery brown hair.

There was the red wool carpet where we kneeled
and the couch above it where our mother sat
to comb our own wet hair.

But my sister taught us on a horse's tail,
thick and black and ethereal,
difficult for a stranger to imagine,
held the strands in her mouth when they became unwieldy,
raked her fingers through the dusty curtain,
as the braid above became more alive and reptilian.

When she wove in each new strand, she wrung out its scent,
dried leaves and grass warming in the sun.

Returning to Water

I watched my first love work a fly rod along the bank of Mossy Creek,
watched him balance the weight of the line—
alive with air and gills and moving water—in the crook of his hand,
watched him hold a fly and breathe it dry between his fingers,
his shoulder blades swimming brown in the sun.
He narrated the movement of trout underwater, and I waited,
wanting the whir and snap of the line, but dreading it, too.
When he spread one out, he would handle her carefully,
dipping his hands into the cool creek water,
so that her scales shone wet, mica in sunlight.
He always released his catch. The fish would pour from his hand like liquid.
I lost her then. No matter how hard I trained my eye on that first flash,
fin returning to water. There was comfort in the disappearing,
as if I knew I, too, would need to find the shadows between reeds,
the belly of that stream, deep and feathery gold, and always moving away.

Kerosene

A summer after sixteen others, unfurls slowly.
You pick Japanese beetles from tomato plants
as the cat winds a warm dust-cover around your ankles,
seal each shimmery insect in a jar of kerosene.
You smell raked alfalfa cooking in the fields.
Your legs swing from the tailgate
as the world rushes by in a shudder of loose gravel.

At night, the boy peels clothing away fragrantly
like pieces of orange,
and you move beneath him inside the sleeping bag,
something almost ready to hatch.
Desire settles in your stomach, thick like pond debris,
and you whisper
don't stop.
But far below, in the valley porch lights wink,
and there is the sound of midnight rigs on Route 33,
distant bees calling you back.

In August, from the porch swing
You watch that calf skid away from its mother, like laughter
skipping through ragweed and clumps of dry orchard grass
to lodge its neck, firmly, in a rusty plow
half-hidden by thistle.
Unnerved by the new weight,
it bolts for the pond.
Your father and the farmer across the road come running,
but it's too late
to pull the thing out alive.

Shadow Story

A woman named Red lived in the stable
where my boyfriend's father housed his horses.
Not the sort of animals I was used to, these were mysterious creatures—
towering, shiny and spotted, bred to rope and race around barrels.
A scent hung thick in that place,
and it was not the same as our barn—
loft stacked high in winter,
floor peppered with mouse droppings and spilled sweet feed,
rotting nests of spooked pigeons,
black mane caught in splinted timber.
His stable was clean and quiet,
the cement floor sprayed daily with water and chemicals.
I did not like that place, but sometimes I let him pull me inside
to kiss against the wall of an empty stall.
It was there he told me how he had seen Red,
crouching below the belly of his father's stallion,
eyes closed, mouth open to take animal inside.
I did not hear his words, but felt them—
breath against my neck and the quiet places inside
me rattling toward it like damp silage.
I looked for her then, wanting to see her face,
to know if it could be true, the words of a seventeen-year-old boy
whose own body twitched nervously beneath my tongue.
I only saw Red once or twice, thick-waisted in a western shirt,
always from behind, a fat braid snaking down her back.
I thought about her sometimes, though, years later,
her shoulders a shadow story,
disappearing through an open doorway.

Unknowns

Cleaning in my father's lab,
I raise each bottle of brown liquid
or lemon-colored powder
and hold it like an Easter egg in my hands
until Dad can read out the name
iodine
sulfur
and I can find a cluster of containers
labeled with the same jumbled letters.

We have been working
through the better part of a Saturday morning,
stirring dust in the windowless light
that hangs around a single yellow bulb,
when I slide a flat cardboard box,
clinking, from the far right corner
of a bottom shelf.
The bottles inside are older
with thick glass and rusting lids.
I hold one up, making the aquamarine swirl
like something alive.

But my father quickly takes that bottle
and the others from me.
Those are the unlabeled chemicals.
They were measured by other professors
who have long since left or died or forgotten,
and now no one knows what's inside
or how reactive it might be.
We have to treat them as if
they're the most powerful of chemicals
because they're the unknowns.
His words are like a fairytale to me.

I think about the strange, cool weight

of my father's gold wrist watch,
the white flutter of his cotton handkerchiefs
folded on the laundry table,
his back bent and palm cupped
to light a cigarette in the wind,
and I know it must be true.

Resurrections

I.
She would fold and unfold the same section,
fearful of the things she didn't yet know she wanted,
leaving the classifieds spread—corners damp and smudged—
like mildew across the bathroom floor,
listening for the words that would help her understand the need:
Walnut chest of drawers, circa 1905, $400;
Antique icebox, original finish, $250;
Farm auction Saturday, 7:00 AM,
livestock, quilts, Depression glass.
Behind the rhythm, sometimes the ache clarified,
became merely a pocket of space inside her
so that, for a moment, she could see herself and what was missing
as clearly as the peaches she skinned and canned each August,
the halved flesh floating in a ball jar, slippery and red-veined,
the pits, darkly grooved, piling in the basin.

II.
She has always understood condition in terms of asking price.
She knows which tables can be sanded and finished,
which ones are covered in cracking veneer.
She knew what it meant when her eldest daughter, just shy of seventeen,
needed two hundred and fifty dollars,
and she would have you believe that is why she called,
why she drove into Runkles Gap with a bag of sweet feed,
why she picked her way through the crabgrass and green briar,
the scar of loose barbed wire snaking out from beneath the deck.
She tells it like she saved him,
tells how his hips and withers rose and played like spoons beneath his skin,
remembers the way his fur—gray with starvation—crackled and split
like kindling under the curry comb,
the way that first week she fed him, only a little at a time,
careful fistfuls of grain.

III.
Look deeper, though, to the act of self-preservation,
the words and the searching and the aging.
Because someone else might never have found the shadowed self,
the palimpsest of blue across the animal's upper lip,
the tattoo that quivers when he noses for corn,
that flicker of color that connects and rises up
like bottle flies from a swished tail.
She traced the animal's history—
a three-year string of losses in races all over the South—
to royal beginnings: blue grass and mint julep, the famous Man-o-War.

The Language of Horses

Her girls knew horses.
First beneath the shroud of a private language,
whinnies softened by sheets and walls,
clack of model ponies along the stairs,
thump of sawdust and squeak of leather,
clatter of bit and bridle hung from a nail on the tack room wall.

For years,
the youngest could only move through the world
on imaginary horses. With a slick willow branch,
she whipped the air and reared back at the edge of the garden.
Through the leafy green tent of pole beans, she galloped.
She named them—these animals no one else could see—
brushed them and snuck them sugar cubes,
had to be convinced to stable them
in the closet for the course of the school day.

Her girls confused horses with people.
One of them hung around the neck of a gelded palomino,
an animal that belonged to an old couple
whose sagging farm seemed ready to sink into the mountains.
She whispered until his ears twitched,
would say only this animal's name
when classmates, with folded bits of paper, tried to predict
the face of her future husband.

The oldest girl went away to ride horses.
They drove her slowly down a dirt road.
She wanted to ask about bug spray,
tampons, sunblock, deodorant,
but the girl rolled down the window and leaned out
toward blue grass and wooden fencing,
said, "That's the smell of horses."
They left her holding a duffle bag,
a hard hat covered in black velvet,

left her to stables and secrets, ice cream every day.
When they returned, it seemed her bangs had grown shaggy,
her figure curvy in just ten days.

Her girls did not fear horses when they should:
broken collar bone, wrist, and finger,
rope burn, toes smashed, coccyx bruised,
knee swollen like a purple cantaloupe.
Only the middle one cowered without reason,
hesitated before lifting a back hoof,
circled wide past the hind end of the aging mare.

Her girls brought boys to see their horses.
They walked with them too long in the woods,
came slinking out from behind the barn.
Her girls felt much and said more than they felt.
It was frightening watching as they shed their childhood,
clumps of fur floating in a cloud, thick and sour off the curry comb.
Their anger, always, was the language of horses,
hair flung wide, words rumbling low in their throats,
the explosion of sound, wild-eyed, snorting and stomping.

And when the girls were gone,
she and their father saw each animal out of this world,
castor oil through a tube when they found the bark of a wild cherry,
bran mash warm in a five gallon bucket.
When gums yellowed and teeth loosened,
she chewed the carrots herself, a constant offering
for the last of their animals resting in her cupped hands.
Then pasture flooded with silence, another hole as large as a van
and rocks piled high behind the barn.

Over the telephone, she told her girls
about the sound, the language of life rising,
told them how it continued to play low inside her head
even after the vet removed the tubes from her ears,
the quiet strumming of a fetal heart, inside
the belly of her new pony stretched wide like a drum.

She said it sounded like rain, like hens scratching,
like walnuts falling in the grass, like wind against a screen,
like the laughter of young girls.

Mapping the Air

I cried in a basement apartment,
open boxes leering.
Outside, the sky lurched above me,
and I shrank like something hunted.
For a day and a half I had been moored to the ground
scrubbing floors and wiping down cabinets,
selecting used furniture from a warehouse across the river.
Alone, I was afraid of so much sky,
longing for Virginia—where the edge of the hollow was a gentle throat
breathing me in, my life till then
a rumble warm in the blue belly of mountains.
But they hadn't left me. Not yet.
They returned, once more, after stopping to hike
the stretch of prairie skirting that college town.
And there, in the space of my doorway
they emptied their pockets, mapping the air
in coneflowers, the feather of a wild turkey, stones
printed with that pale lichen I would come to know so well.

Mother's Wishes

When she was a girl in Kansas,
she searched the summer fence lines

because the wind blew things to her,
magazines, broken umbrellas, a twenty dollar bill.

Now I, too, know this place and can imagine
her neighborhood: sighing porches, cord grass, Euonymous hedges,

and the fences—chain links and pickets
crying before a thunderstorm—

the things people plant to anchor themselves
beneath so much sky.

I can see her running along a row of cottonwoods
as they shimmer and turn the silver bellies of their leaves,

surrendering to August and cloud cover,
the gray-green haze, moisture like a mouth

against the glass of a prairie town.
There would be heat, the chorus of locusts scattering

amidst her footfall. Now I walk
each morning, and my eyes scan the hedge rows,

still seeking my mother's wishes—
what she asked the wind for and what she failed to find.

In the Outer Banks

The Carolina marsh breathes all around us,
and our bicycles, borrowed relics with balloon tires
hiss across the sandy pavement.
We swim through the twilight calm,
so unlike the cold Atlantic
we watched pound the shore earlier in the afternoon.
Leaving our bikes in the brush,
we enter an open construction site and lie down,
enveloped in a cool pocket of sand,
the skeleton of a new beach house
rising around us, monumental.
Finished houses glitter
like lit Jack-o-Lanterns in the distance,
and shadowed figures move
across their bright windows.

Last December, I walked to your place,
through the silence of the year's first snow,
to write a message with the toe of my boot
in the whiteness collecting beneath your lit window—
I must have seen it in a movie.
Inside, I found your apartment filled with male voices
and the windows steamed with laughter.
I was relieved when, upon leaving,
I saw my rash words covered in fresh snow.

Now I wish I could see the words between our faces
finally exhaled into Kansas cold.
I don't want to lose your voice here,
in the scent of sawdust and myrtle blossom.
I imagine when we finally rise
we will leave the shape of us
together in the sand.

Winter and Homesick

I.
December in Phoenix,
I drink dryness from the air,
watch the men at the VFW pull hoses
to wet trees shipped down from Oregon.
Here memory is physical and startling,
like the taste of nose bleed feathering against ones throat.
Somewhere, four girls move through a patch of cedar,
ancient pasture reclaimed by forest,
thick with undergrowth, even in winter,
the movement of snow and brush and ritual
traced across time, toboggans, hand-knitted, in a line of red.

II.
The sparkly haze of glass beneath a streetlamp,
a man's hand in the small of my back,
palm trees—voices in silhouette—
and the thump of an upright rising from some basement bar.
I wished for what I couldn't articulate,
searched for it, shoulders muscled and skin pricked,
the way I now move through AM radio
after the sound of old country,
records my parents played Saturday evenings.

III.
In Virginia my father feeds deer,
slices twine with a pocket knife carved from antler,
watches each bale accordion in the scent of summer.
He scatters orchard grass along the edge of the woods
where white-tail deer sniff the snow each evening,
willing them out of the twilight,
their hoof prints dark fingers of memory,
because home, always a little further, hovers
below the surface of winters everywhere.

Rise

To fight loneliness, a farm girl will rise early.
She'll wake when the trains
rumble through the desert suburbs.
Inside her tank top, a plastic bag of baby carrots
swinging heavy and cool
as she jogs through the silver light,
the palm trees gray and foreign,
already the sun off the asphalt,
the breeze like a hair dryer against the back of her legs.
The canal will whisper and reflect,
while smooth drum, scales latticed and prehistoric,
swim in the shadow of the cement wall.
Soon the animals expect her, and she'll imagine
them watching as she crosses Broadway and turns
onto that section of street where apartments give way
to ranches. The horses will lean over the fence,
stamp and snort and snake their heads.
She will stand in the ditch, feed them one carrot at a time,
let them nuzzle her palms after the bag is empty.
Hours later, back in her apartment,
there is still the sweet tang of fur off her hands.

Monsoon Season

All that morning we followed summer,
the slow course of a trickling stream
though tall pines, then a grove of aspen,
trunks almost silver in June sunlight.
Talk thinned by the time we reached
the meadow, perhaps half a mile across,
and we moved separately through that open space,
spreading into green like a fistful of tossed gravel.
Clouded Sulphurs hovered there,
and they moved over the water like lace.
We fell silent during the ascent, the scramble
over boulders, the felled skeleton of an upturned spruce.

The cutbank rose beneath our feet,
clarifying the way time carves space,
even through that shelf of igneous,
which once ran hot, which glows still,
according to local tribes, who story that peak
female and golden, always
anchored in the ground by a yellow beam of sun,
a core of warm abalone.

Yet all was shadow that afternoon,
as the trail narrowed and the temperature dropped.
I wondered if you—how many paces behind me?—
could feel it too. Change in pressure,
electricity charging the little hairs along your forearms.

When I broke out of the tree line again,
the sky had thickened overhead,
clouds purple and saturated, like blood rising
beneath bruised skin. And I felt just that way—
suddenly tender. Even before lightening crackled,
we turned together and ran. Did you feel it too?
How the ground fell away and we rose up,

how we cleared something more than
clumps of sedge and crumbling stone?

I wasn't myself again until we reached that meadow.
Even there, we could see lightening strike the open ground.
As we made our final, frantic push, the aspens had all turned
their leaves belly-up in surrender, and by the time we reached the car,
I knew something had spun inside us, too. The rain was pelting the windows,
drawing the scent of vanilla off the bark, and your mouth
was moving against mine like something burrowing out of darkness.

A Fingerprint, Carried Long and Quiet
    for Jessie

This summer, I walked to my sister's,
breath of an early shower hovering,
oiled branches whispering,
and I felt the landscape like a childhood language,
sunlight across the web of a yellow silk spider,
a fingerprint, carried long and quiet.

I knew, suddenly, life was here,
knew like any animal, wet-nosed and quivering
in the smell of black dirt and dead leaves,
ditch water, kudzu holding fast,
the bark of so many white oaks.

I spread my arms to that pocket of forest
still rooted and reaching,
felt the rattle of other lives through the undergrowth.
My mountains, hundreds of miles away,
yet so close, and a girl child growing inside my sister.

Like a leaf arching toward water,
my heart turned on the axis of morning,
thankful for earth absorbed through pores,
for sky and senses peppered in a wake of rising starlings.

Blessing, North of Perigueux

Morning comes, silver, fog hanging low,
gossamer along a river valley in southwest France.
You sit on your pack and watch young horses scatter across the field below.
Stopping just short of the limestone wall, they are all light and angle,
and it seems they should rise up, curl like autumn leaves on the next lip of air.
In a few hours you will enter a cave four miles north of this place,
and then you will know why cedar lined fields
and the faces of your sisters are here
whispering a blessing against the back of your skull.
Your eyes will follow the glow of a red pin light across millennia,
and your mind, slowly, will reconcile each image—
bear, water, piece of night sky.
But when your guide leads you into the deepest room,
the face of rock once reserved for only the most sacred shapes,
recognition will float up your spine, neck hair rising,
a prayer for horses and people, in which you will remember this moment,
morning and mares grazing along the hillside,
a cathedral, glazed in an arm of early sun.

I, Who Finally Dissolved

Little Deaths: Jackie Kennedy Explains her Composure to the American Public

You want to milk my suffering
as if I were a viper, enough antidote
to nurse this entire country
warm inside my painted mouth.

When the berm holds, you fish
suspicion out of the stop-bath—
my suit like peppermint, my wig suddenly
obvious, blood spots on my hem.

What you don't suspect: I wanted
only to hold his head in place
for the moment it took
to say goodbye just as I was

permitted to hold our first daughter—
palm her gray cheek, run my finger
tip along the points of her quiet
spine, barely formed.

Patrick, the one who would
meld us into recognition again.
Though he survived two days,
would you believe I never held him
living, only heard his cry?

And the others—didn't you
know?—I held them in my own way.
A subject no lady should raise,
not even at home, but I have many times
touched that same rusted loss
in the crux of my panties.

So well a wife already knows the stillness

of her husband's breath and pulse.
Often, I watched the jagged flutter
of that pale triangle of flesh
hidden to you by his collar, and
always I saw the same skin settle.
I have resurrected this love before,
Dei Gratia. But a delicate seam
can be stitched only a few times.

You want to crack it like a book cover
shoddily printed, but a mother
knows how to read grief then turn it aside,
so that it might feather, become
merely a page in a much longer story.

At My Desk, Ten Weeks Pregnant

It is good that I write
because already I know
what it is to labor
each day for perfection,
shrouded
in the certainty
that beauty and truth are linked
intricately
at the cellular level.
No matter
that I cultivate each ritual
and shun each vice.
Creation is still a gift,
a yolk bobbing uncertainly
inside a fragile shell.
I'm still waiting
for these words to crackle
like dry sticks.
I'm still just filling my own lungs.

Thinking of My Mother, 28 Years and Six Months

When I think of my mother and picture how she was
at the age I am now, I think of waiting,
of her in a two piece suit, skirted in gauzy yellow and pink,
a plastic pool and a romance novel,
pages breathing and feathering
as she fans them against her thumb.
These were ours, stretches of afternoon
before my younger sister, still diapered and sour,
rose from the crib and cried through the screened window,
before the bus lumbered up the road.
The rumble of bees over dandelion, the sigh of the cornfield.
What did she think as she watched me
sort pebbles into careful piles? Such cultivated silence.
If she rolled onto her stomach, I would hover
and try to count the moles on her back.

Pica

For three nights during the first trimester,
I dream of eating an enormous white candle.
With each bite, wax turns to sweet cream in my mouth.

As I eat, I walk through our house
fingering the artifacts of this wide life we've fashioned together:
pottery from that fishing town in Connemara;
the bowl we brought back from the desert,
carved from Juniper and inlaid with turquoise;
novels waiting in ready stacks, bedside and along the bar;
laptops recharging on opposite ends of the dining room table,
like bookends or, perhaps, more like dueling pianos.
In the dark kitchen, the lurid glow of new appliances.

Outside, although it is December, cricket song burns in the tall grass.
I sit on the cement stoop, taking bite after bite,
holding each mouthful of wax heavy on my tongue,
letting it melt down my throat in a strange, private Eucharist.

The next week, I come across the chapter
in one of those glossy parenting books.
Seeing it on paper, I am reminded—instant, wet-mouth, dry-gut
need—the word suddenly endowing my subconscious cravings
with definition. It might have been clay I hungered for,
or ash, laundry starch, even chipped paint.

I think of well water running cold
from the tap of my parents' farmhouse,
and I know where I am now matters less than where I come from:
the rural south. Like any tributary, I rush away from my source.
But ground covered can never compare to mineral depth,
and I can't help but wonder
what waking appetites will soon rear their heads.

Dry Leaves

I run across the face of the autumn moon
while limestone and skeletons of old barns stretch
below. Letters swirl from my hair like dry leaves,
float with November and the smell of wood smoke.

While limestone and skeletons of old barns stretch
long shadows across the moonlit valley, I watch words rise
to float with November and the smell of wood smoke
like thick clouds climbing the hoar-frosted hollow.

Away from shadow, above the moonlit valley, I watch, wise
with slumber's understanding. From the sky, art is smaller
yet clout thick with design as the hoar-frost and hallowed
in farm's warm ritual—hay bales which spring open

after tumbling down from the loft. Art is smaller even
than rolls rising on the table or kindling on the stoop.
Farm's warm ritual: quiet seeds which spring will open
into clamoring vines, pollen the wind will lift and settle—

an old, shimmery fable brindling the back stoop.
I run across the face of autumn with the moon
inside my clamoring voice. When I wake, I will sift letters
from the sky until my words crack the air like dry leaves.

Divination

Six months pregnant, returning from the pool
you encounter three boys bent over the base
of a Palo Verde, shoulders tense with the thrill.
They prod unraveling wisps of Yucca, striking
then drawing back to wait. Their laughter rises
sharp, sound reduced to its quick
like the bark of a chained dog.

Fourteen weeks since, through fear-
scented blood, he revealed himself to you.
And you would have known, even without
the arrow marking what the technician called *the turtle*
there on the foggy screen. Something
in his eyes—almond shaped like his father's.

Moments ago, poolside in a lounge chair,
you were reading Louise Erdrich, imagining
sunlight streaming magenta inside your womb.
Soon, you will do what you do each morning:
spread your mat and move through a series
of Hatha postures choreographed
to the sound of the Mid-Atlantic shore,
but this child, he only churns
to life when a low rider thumps
hip-hop from the curb.

And now these boys—their hair shining
in that pure desert light. *What are you doing?*
Not a scorpion or black widow, though
both sometimes scuddle across the travertine
back in your condominium—
Grandaddy, three-legs-shy, still trying
to climb the slick, gray-green bark.
Don't you know that's how serial killers get their start?

Flint-edged, yours is a voice hard
to recognize, and when they turn to smile—
gap-toothed, dimpled—the Sonoran sky
is a vein of turquoise drawn into relief
by their radiant, upturned faces.

Dark Moon
    For Boyd

You would wait for the waning,
though neighbors and bank tellers
and the young man stacking cantaloupe in Country Mart
all swore you would come sooner.
The woman at the counter of Braum's dairy bar,
eyeing the planetary curve of my white T-shirt,
the swollen plain of my bare feet,
begged me to lie down, for just a moment,
in a vinyl booth before walking home.
Even your father, on the morning the midwife had calculated—
July 29, the Full Buck Moon, high summer,
when the antlers of White Tails, after weeks of twisting up
in their own form of quickening, finally push out from their foreheads—
even he hovered in the doorway, sighing,
while I sanded and painted the floor.

Animals will wait,
And because of that, I should have known,
should have remembered the way a sheep, stretched,
beneath the heavy growth of the season's wool,
as tight and round as an iron cistern,
would always wait until the March sky swallowed the moon,
until the pale face receded, leaving only cold, fierce
pricks of starlight and steam rising from wet nostrils,
before dropping her slick lamb to the half-frozen ground.
Animals know the power of dark time, that secret corner of days
when, on spindle legs, the young begin to suckle.

What would I have given,
a week later, for pure darkness,
for the scent of damp leaves, for a pocket of tall grass?
Each shuffling revolution around the hospital's air conditioned hallway
led past a window where would I let go

of your father's shoulders to press my hands and face against the glass
which held onto the warmth of August deep into that night.
Far below, a bed of Tick-seed shivered,
the blooms reaching and bowing like tiny stemmed suns.
Overhead, the moon was a cervix opening the sky—
a waning crescent, the color of old bone, and just as hard,
like the sliver of horn I had palmed
weeks before in the Wichita Mountains.

Each time your father
touched my shoulder and drew me back into step,
you rocked against my spine, a boulder gathering
weight for the final surrender to gravity.
Hours later, panting and squatting,
had I that pale trinket, or any smooth stone,
I could have worried it into air.
But instead, it was I who finally dissolved
only to be reformed a thousand times
by your breath.

Winter Without

Blackwork Solstice: Mary Tudor, July 1555

The women gathered here have begun to whisper.
Dark silk through pale linen: they pull the thread
with such fervor. Suspicion rattles the damp air
without cease, just as rain pelts the stained glass.

Dark silk through pale linen: they spread kohl
across powdered skin that I might face another day.
Without cease, just as rain pelts the stained glass,
I plea to Saint Margaret: draw forth the pain

across tightened skin that I might face another day.
When trapped beneath labor's heaves, I will still
plea to Saint Margaret: draw forth the pain.
My heart flutters in my chest like blackbirds

rain-trapped beneath the eaves. I will still
when this smock and kirtle phantom-float and a babe's
heart flutters against my chest. Like blackbirds
gathering, Philip's dark beard will descend

when this smock and kirtle phantom-float. A babe
to wrap and rock, tenderness to stave famine's
gathering. Philip's dark bared, your will descend
in the conjoined cries of mother and child.

Rap and rock tender sheaves to stave famine.
Sunlit villagers will thatch the rotted roofs.
In the conjoined cries of mother and child,
a holy kingdom calmed with an heir's promise.

Past sunlit villages' newly thatched roofs,
the men will return from muddy encampments—
a holy kingdom come with the air's promise,
if only something lies beneath this farthingale.

Yea, the men return from muddy encampments,
and the women gathered have begun to whisper—
they perceive only lies beneath this farthingale.
With such fervor, suspicion rattles the damp air.

Viable: A Letter Confessing My Lack of Faith to My Newborn Son

Last January,
in the minute and a half it took
the ultrasound technician to pronounce that word,
hours after I stood up from the sofa
and felt the blood rush warm out of me,
I thought about the moments
when knowledge of your life was mine alone,
when I had sat, heart-pounding,
holding the confirmation of your presence inside me,
frozen, unable or unwilling, to rise and begin
the inevitable process of sharing you.

I thought about the pills
my sister had taken months before,
locked in the bathroom, her head bowing
to drink from the faucet, again and again.
Rain pouring off the eaves like quicksilver,
a windowed tunnel in Dulles International Airport.
Past midnight, driving south on I81,
I never turned on the radio,
certain, only through silence,
would I know if something changed,
if she opened her eyes, or
if the steady sound of the respirator
suddenly failed to sustain her.

I thought about children erased,
when my sister was young, already struggling
to tread the secret undercurrents of her illness,
the ones I had, until you, failed to consider
in terms other than my own immediate loss—
my parents, preoccupied, whispering in the kitchen,
money no longer spent on school clothes—
the ones I had, even as a grown woman, an aunt,

come to view simply as statistical fall out.
And I thought about the times I flirted,
with that possibility—breathless and spread
across an unfolded sleeping bag in the back of a Chevy S10,
the earth beneath my skin freshly tilled to the surface,
by night air and a boy's fingers,
my body suddenly ready to absorb anything.

I thought about the choice sometimes involved,
my grandfather in an electric hospice bed,
the cancer which began in his lymphatic system
now pulsing steadily through his body.
Weeks of silence, his breath
quieter, even, than the humid sigh of White Oaks
just outside, until the morning he rose up on his elbows,
called my mother in from the kitchen.
"There are some people here," he said,
"some people who want me to go with them."
My mother asked the only question she could,
"Papa, do you want to go?"
And he answered—"Yeah"—just before his breathing ceased,
"Yeah. I think I do."

I thought about the times I took it so lightly,
somehow forgot to value survival at all:
The summer I played with kids on a neighboring farm,
wading into the shifting mountain of silage
that steamed heady and deep inside a warm silo.
Fifteen, delivering meals to shut-ins—
no seatbelt, limbs sticking to cracked leather,
rattle of gravel and ditch weed,
the smell of scotch across the front seat of a red Studebaker convertible,
and the hands of that church elder, damp and shaking
against the antique steering wheel.
Or, the night I drove a carload of rowdy teenagers,
windows open to dry August evening,
a sling shot passed around, quarter sticks of dynamite
sizzling into open pasture.

I want to say I knew your heart was still beating,
I want to say that your father and I passed the certainty of you
back and forth between our clasped hands
like a warm electrical current,
that together we felt your presence,
that we knew you were there, a surge of power
through a green sapling pressed to a hot fence.

I should have known
because I have seen it before,
the way life can inexplicably root and shimmer:
the damp track of a mountain lion marking a Sonoran wash,
Chestnut saplings still sprouting through wet leaves,
my sister's first born, his pink fingers uncurling like a bright starfish.
But, at the time, all I could see was the trajectory
rising up from the darker corners of my subconscious,
your life, mere weeks, burning down,
a sudden explosion in the summer night,
skid marks rutted in a back road,
sunlight disappearing
as the hatch opens and the ground gives way.

Phantom

Over a period of months,
the neighbor's English bulldog
Jezebel grows fat and slow.
She clears her bowl of kibble
and then eats her way
into the bag behind
the laundry room door.
Evenings, she flops
on the driveway, panting,
swollen teats rising
black and rubbery
from her brindled fur.

When she begins to drag
towels and old newspaper
into the shadows of the crawl space,
fashioning a birthing den,
a vet is consulted who
under the cruel blanket of anesthesia,
removes the animal's uterus.

Upon waking, Jezebel whines
and searches beneath the house.
Soon her appetite wilts until
she refuses to tongue even cheese
from our open palms. She is gone
within a matter of weeks, just
as I knew she would be.

After the First Miscarriage

We lie in bed all afternoon,
my head in the crook of your arm,
the way we lay as newlyweds
when only the long press of our bodies
anchored us inside each hour.
My face grows hot and damp against your shirt.
Our crying steams the bedroom windows.
Outside, rain screeches,
metallic through the gutters,
spills onto winter grass.
And I think how
if it were just two degrees colder,
this would all be snow.

Bunraku: On the Feast of the Epiphany

The three kings are here this morning,
amazed expressions frozen in papier-mâché,
bodies—draped linen and cotton—
planted in far corners of the sanctuary.
Possible, at first, to overlook them,
if not for Father Al's smile which twitches
and threatens to break through the gospel.

I stand Boyd on my knees as their dance begins,
and soon he is the inanimate one, body stretched taut,
the slow, lumbering journey of the puppets quieting
even the pulse of his thumb in his mouth.
Can it be that I, too, am holding my breath?

Life amplified in the sheer scale,
in the connections necessary to ignite movement.
Each trinity of puppeteers reaches and bends,
and each king moves forward, lurching then gliding.
There is something elephantine in their procession,
something of groaning hardwood trees, something even
of Boyd's own first wavering steps.

We have been moving just this way—three as one—
for nearly as many years, and now
we await our own private manifestation:
In two days, another ultrasound, to confirm the presence
of Boyd's sibling, the remaining twin
in a pair already half-vanished.

Is that why something gathers in my throat now
that the three kings have reached the alter, why I am
blinking back my own glistening veil
as a baby I have often seen slung close to the breast
of his mother there in the back row
is drawn forward, wriggling and warm-bodied,

as each Magi, in turn, bows?

In a few moments, we will do what has become
our own ritual of hope—we will retreat to the chapel
and light a candle of Boyd's choosing, focus on that flame
until it becomes a single, unwavering star
beneath the force of our small prayers.
I want to let that light and this dance flicker
in my chest through the coming days,
but I know how epiphanies spark in the world outside.
How many times have I stood before my students
to explicate those final paragraphs of "The Dead"?
I know light always creates shadow,
flame burns as often as it warms.

Conflagration

Lent, and the church is stripped bare,
save that purple cassock.
Gone the incense, warm wax
off the advent wreath.

And for the first time
I wonder what they do
with all the evergreen boughs—
do they burn them
like palm leaves in the spring?

quia pulvis es, et in pulverem reverteris

Wednesday—still bleeding,
still cramping—
for the first time in a decade,
I did not receive ashes,
did not anticipate and record
my sacrifice in a leather-bound notebook.
The absurdity of abstaining now
from chocolate or soda,
of arranging only midday
crackers and fruit on a dessert plate.
Haven't I given up
enough?

    Bathwater drains pink.
    Fistfuls of hair clog the drain.

doleutis animae eleyson

Here, inside the chapel,
winter sunlight becomes insult
through the prism of stained glass.
Head bowed toward tabernacle,

I still feel the power that hums there
like corona discharge over dry grass.
Oh, that I could have locked the lives of my unborn
in a twelfth century box, swallowed
the tiny, rattling iron key.

    Anger is hot and brittle.
    It would only take a spark.

    doleutis animae eleyson
How does one survive
to be pulled from the oven alive?
Hell is an inferno, the Holy Spirit
a tongue of red flame.

Proof: To My Doubting Husband
    for Gus and Ann

I. Statement
Geometry was the only math I was
ever any good at.

I am.

That's what I tell the CVS manager
who, after scanning yet another box test,
asks, "Which is it?
Are you hoping or are you worrying?"

I am.

II. Given
Let the twenty nine positives—
two-a-day
since the first, which appeared just hours
before that clot, the size of
a silver dollar,
a dwarf sun—
equal one
remaining.

"Well, there's nothing left."
He wanted me to recognize it
as empty, that doctor,
after the phantom pregnancy
three months before. So he pointed
to the dusky triangle on the monitor
anchored in the wall—
"The endometrium doesn't even appear
particularly thick."
His attempts at condolence:

"Once again, you may never have been
pregnant—home tests can be hard to read.
And even if you were, you're thirty-five,
which makes this kind of loss more common.
Up to twenty percent of pregnancies end
this way. You'll go on to have more babies."

Asshole.
Let the sticks I've taped inside
this manila folder—fifty-eight
pink lines—
equal one
remaining.

If you must wait for more
blood tests, the exponential doubling
of HCG, so be it. But let me celebrate
the one
remaining.
Watch me hang these tests on our Christmas tree.

III. Reasoning
Remember how, weeks ago, two stars fell
as we drove home through Rarity Mountain pass.
I heard you gasp as each
dazzling line etched the black windshield.

Consider what the French Canadian palm reader told me
long before I even knew you,
fifteen years ago in a room behind
a bar on a Montreal side street:
"You will conceive twins."

Believe this:
For three days, my breasts were electric—
no other way to say it. A bug-zapper

concealed under that blue dress
until someone pulled the plug.
Nothing for two days, and then
this current surging again
against the rough
cotton of my T-shirt.

IV. Conclusion
You will believe
what I know to be true
too late, only after
the midwife confirms everything.

Weeks after the gestational sac,
    that pale galaxy,
comes into view.

Only a week before the heart beat stops.
Only a fortnight before the bleeding.

Fifty days after I knew.

And still forty more until I pass
the placenta,
pinkish gray and wrinkled,
    like the folded ear of some animal.

I will call you from the bathroom
stall on the second floor
of the Keene-Johnson building
to tell you

exactly what I'm holding in my hand.

After the Second Miscarriage

He doesn't cry until a cardinal
slams into the back door.
He covers her with a cardboard box
because he can't stand to see
the brown plumage, heaving
against the frost. What finally moves
my husband's rigid grief is the bird's mate:
that drop of red marking our fence line
long after she is in the ground.

Winter Without

A skim of ice covers the lake this morning,
rotting leaves shining gray
in the brittle light along the shore.
January, and a few osage oranges
still clot the frozen mud.
Hardwoods pale as old bone.

We have come again to walk the loop
because I am following, as literally as possible,
my mother's advice: day by day,
one foot in front of the other.
How to proceed when only cliché endures?

I search the frosted ground
for an object I might hold up for my son—
bright boy, strapped safe on my back,
the only one who remains—
for he still needs to hold the world
at arm's length, to shake magic down
as snow from a globe.
But this month the tracks of field mice are strange cuneiform
snaking beneath the bridge.

I would like to uncover a stone,
warm it in my hands to anchor us
deep in this world.
I would like to fashion a needle from a sliver of ice,
close the seam on this emptiness
that still pulses within me.

But nothing—
not even that skein of geese
clearing the tree line—
can stitch me whole.

Bajada

After six months, I drove back to the desert like a lover.
    December. In the wake of a slow, winter rain.

Week-old grass curled back into the sand
    like the golden fur of some sleeping animal.

A few leaves still clung to the spiked rods of ocotillo, gray-green, desperate
    like the tongues of cats.

Those already fallen darkened the base of each plant
    in reverent, measured shadows.

My eyes followed cutbanks washed into the earth
    by the season of my absence,

hoping for some sign of forgiveness—the slip of a coyote
    across the highway.

The smell is never the same.

I wanted to separate the air into parts,
    dedicate my breath to each one—

Mesquite, Resurrection Moss, Mormon Tea—
    spread them in front of me like colors on a spectrum.

I knew then that identification is the same as love,
    another word for possession,

and I remembered what I had seen years before
    and hours south of that place—

the nests of pack rats beneath a sandstone overhang
    clotted with fur and stones and waste,

twigs bleached like pale bones,
    yucca curling in dry ribbons.

As night rose up out of the sand,
    I looked for a place I knew,

the dusky splay of soil and volcanic rock
    where the ridge folded and slid into the desert floor,

and something thickened inside my chest when I couldn't find it.

For Her to Enter This World

These Terrible Times: The Angel of the House Resurrected, 1941

How I would love to believe
that sound is the scratching of my pen
drawing ink from the well, carving this page into something true.

Or even robins returning to nest beneath the eaves,
but two weeks into March, the twigs gathered last spring molder
like old thatch. Song birds are fewer this year,
though I watch for a flash of red along the garden hedge.

Instead, it is Her footfall which marks the hours,
incessant as the great clock. All winter
She strained to flush me out of the brush.
I hoped the rain would drown her, leave only wet
pieces strewn like leaves along the river path.

But I hear Her this very moment…
    sniffing around the hyacinth bed.

Once I was sheltered here,
though She could rise from any damp corner in Monk House.
Back then, She merely shook tarnished silver in the drawers,
lifted linen panels into taunting sails
so that every sunbeam cradled winking dust motes.
She would alight, for a moment, beneath the largest oak
to make evening settle like amber around my nephew's shoulders.

But now She has begun to claw at the walls of this lodge,
loosening the shingle, until even my ideas start to unhinge—I fear I will
lose them all, like fevered teeth, like pearls
snapped from a thread and rolling the parlor floor.

Years ago, I joked that I had killed Her,
but war can resurrect as well as destroy—
even those bren gun trenches along Mount Caburn

offer green shards of bronze, pieces of an Iron Age pendant
which will be strung like a prayer flag in the vault of the British Museum.

I should be safe at last
from the heat which simmered all those years,
dancing Redowa with the moon. I thought I could
burn the desire out of my womb, tear it like an errant page,
but it creeps back: that vine the gardener calls Bittersweet—
ever loosening the knit of the dry stone wall.
What is writing but an act of parturition?

I feed each life. I swaddle and comfort.
When imagination stirs, it is I
who have cast light on the spider's silver web.
I suffer, and I lift my own feet to plunge
over the edge. I follow beyond what shatters,
all the way into the ground.

Yet critics insist on tracing fragile lines back to expired lovers—
they sketch Clarissa on rice paper and hold her up to Madge.

These days, the air is full of smoke and supplication—
the very things on which She feasts. It might have been
She who blasted the roof from the Mecklenburgh flat.
At the very least, She wields dust and rubble as a private snare.

Listen to that iron key rattling the latch…
    it flutters like an injured sparrow.

And then suddenly She dares feign absence
when I know She is underfoot, curled like a feather
in the shadows of my skirt. She sighs and passes through me,
wraith-like, yet the narrow bridge groans beneath our weight.

More and more, I wish for smooth stones
Thoby and I gathered from the strand below Tallund House.
I remember how we placed them along the stoop,
stacked them in our own mysterious language.

We tasted the salt which graced their surfaces
just the same as it did our skin,
the world's edges reduced to briny memory—
so much which water can remove. I would like
to feel that perfect weight again, an anchor
in these terrible times, something I could keep
like a talisman, deep in the pocket of my coat.

Prayer from Cedar Creek Falls

Up here at the end of August
when this stream has narrowed
to a cool trickle,
the sound of water is memory.
Let me wet my fingers.
Let me suck a warm stone.
Let me simply listen—
for that is the fastest way
to move into light
or toward shadow.
Both flicker here—in low water,
in spaces behind rock.
A wood thrush divides the hour,
and I am captured sand—sinking.
Absence holds heat like exposed rock,
rises to flutter against the back of my skull
like those sulphurs weaving
through the sunlight downstream,
and in that haze is the real fear.
I've heard water likened to laughter, or silver,
or, even, breaking glass.
Let me hear it as breath,
that intake of air that trails surprise,
so I can live around the knowledge
that less is always more,
that there is no distance
between loss and love.

For Her to Enter This World: Hopscotch House, December 2010

Deer sniff the snow outside my window each evening,
and come morning, like softened scars, their tracks
cross sunlit pasture. I am able here
to follow the paths of wild things

into winter brush, always careful
to turn back when my abdomen tightens,
though at thirty-two weeks such labor is practice,
simply another form of quickening. My world here

is contracted, as well: husband and son grown small,
a spit of land viewed through a spy glass.
Still, I cannot help but train my eye on those distant
rocks. I step firmly—the rimed porch steps

glistening. At my desk, I trace these letters
into a constellation on which to course the coming
weeks. Sheltered by my quiet body, my daughter begins
to move again. Here, she speaks only to me, marking

the damp soil of my ribs, playing the splayed spoons
of my creaking hips. In the dark, voices fill
this empty house. I'm not sure I believe
in ghosts. But that light which flashes above

the mantle as I court sleep, surely it is a form
of knocking—they are back, the ones that bled
from me this time last winter. They suspect
what I know: already she has begun to snuff the flame

of that throbbing. What will become of their names
once I palm her dark hair, once I bow to her needy mouth?
I will rub their bones into fire. For her
to enter this world, so much must be sacrificed

to gods I don't understand. I will pull
long hairs from my brush. I will shake
crusts from my plate. I will ask winter birds
to carry gifts wherever they roost.

Moving Water
    For Maeve

From the start, you knew
how to fool us: surviving
in separate parts, past
the days we checked off the calendar,
beginning before we were permitted
to anticipate you. Our joy—
that the body knew
better than doctors or books,
better than our own indulgent despair,
knew, before we did,
when the switch was thrown,
and at the cellular level
hope could gleam once more.

Let that word include
you, let it include God, let it
include desire, as well
as desire's quiet child,
let it include the parts of all
of us, your father and I, all
of us existing as pure
light, as moving water.

That you would come quickly
should have been clear.
For one thing, there was no time
for photographs, no weekly record
like the one chronicling your brother's growth,
black Sharpie on white card stock,
make-shift sign beneath an ever growing bump,
only the cast attempted weeks after
the date recommended, so that you dropped
even as your father and brother, trying

to suspend growth in a perfect tableau,
smoothed strips of wet gauze
across my greased middle.

Perhaps every second child knows
she must hurry, knows surprise
is the only way to deconstruct
the delicate balance which precedes her.
Now you wield the same
power, running as I call
your name, sliding
behind filmy curtains,
folding yourself beneath
the bathroom counter.

The afternoon of your birth,
while your brother poured warm
bathwater over my belly, outside
an early thaw was brewing.
On the way to the hospital,
sunlight split February wide open,
casting a luminescence over the pastures—
everywhere, cattle coming in to feed.

At that rural hospital,
submerged in the birthing pool,
this time, I knew
I would have to give myself over,
the same way, once, as a toddler
splashing along the edge of the Atlantic,
when my hand slipped out of my father's,
I gave myself over to drowning,
hung between worlds as foam churned overhead.

Don't forget we are
the same. I know
your wet rush, girl child,
have ridden it myself—

turning clothing aside
like the pages of a book,
raising my thumb to hail unknown
cars, opening my mouth
to one boy and then another,
to someone's hash pipe, to words
I wish I hadn't. Why
are the regrets of my
past already poured
into those of your future?

In the end, water loosened my bones—
not the stream filling the tub and steaming
the mirror, cradling that body no longer mine,
not even the vial of holy water sealed
inside my suitcase, although I would anoint
your dark head later that evening,
but those mysterious currents we already shared.
Before them, I opened suddenly
as I couldn't for your brother,
like the calm surface of a lake
pricked by a barn swallow, by a shard
of thrown glass. I rippled wide
so that you might shine forth, tinkling
with spring-melt through the eaves.

By the time we drove you home,
just two days later,
the creeks had risen past their banks,
and the route back could never be
the same.
Just look how the roadside blossoms
in your presence, Jonquils and Forsythia
shattering winter's gray fence lines.

Your Pulse

The Work of Women: Sarah Wakes to an Empty House

Like breathing sand—
the boy's absence
swirls sleep-stale air
until I cannot fill my lungs.
I rise to shake
his empty bedding
and hear
the clatter of animals
carved from juniper,
the companions an only child
curls into his blankets.

The two of them might
have gone to gather wood,
allowing an old woman
to sleep and still
fire unleaven loaves
before the risen sun snuffs
the sound of olive leaves,
the scent of water.

But something else
draws them up the slope
into the gray light,
where I see
them moving now,
one hand shading my eyes,
the other gripping my keffiyeh.
The sun catches the blade
at my husband's side,
and fear cinches my throat,
tightens my limbs—
as suddenly as flax knots
when I shift the loom.

He whose name we dare not
speak—Abraham claims
He will spin generations
from the rough skein of this sand.
But what can a man know
of lonely?
Not as much as I
who have witnessed blood
wrung from the constant moon
and then the woman
who pounded those stains from the linen
drawn into my husband's arms,
a horizon that failed
to settle into home.

I will utter those syllables now,
not to beseech His intervention,
but to challenge His claim
on what can only really be mine:
He may have rooted
life into a tarnished womb,
but it was I who pushed
the boy into this world,
teeth clinched
against a sprig of pennyroyal
as my body split like grapes
overripe on the vine.

Hallal,
Abraham will say,
when he returns, eyes shining—
the sunlit splash
from the waterskin
clearing the wall of the well.
I won't remind him
that even bulls pulled by brass rings
are released to drink from the spring
before entering temple gates—

beasts never catch
the scent of fig and pine
until the knife is drawn
and the stones are slick.

In the coming days,
I will devise my own rituals
into a new covenant:
moving the lamp
and my husband's sandals
once his breath settles into sleep,
doubling the dalet knot
for the guarantee
of his sputter and curse
should he rise early.
But first my boy,
his dark, trembling lashes,
his face pale and smooth as millet
which the two of us, mother and son,
will grind throughout the morning
because I will insist today
that he help me prepare bread—
the work of women.
That he might lean into my shoulder
as we kneel before the mortar,
That I might, for a moment,
when we rise,
take each of his hands
in mine, if only
to brush the flour from his palms.

A Large Body of Water
    Gloria Jones and Willard Plentl, Galveston, 1938

They stand, in the days,
when you could drive a car onto the sand
or fire up an oil drum for surfcasting,
on a nearly emptied beach,
his arm around her shoulders,
hers anchoring his waist. Deep
in the background, kids cluster
around some artifact the gulf
has deposited on the strand.

Shiver-ribbed and spring-limbed,
hip grazing the island's first nylon swimsuit—
his gift to her on her eighteenth birthday—
he laughs at the camera, but she is focused.

Decades later, we will joke about how
she cultivated two looks for photographs:
the charming head tilt and the don't-you-dare-
snap-that-shot.

But here her face is singular—
generations commence in that gaze—
though he will have to woo her still.

Perhaps the woman always decides.
That is why the redbird alights
on the branch outside her window.

The water that afternoon would have been
sun-struck, dappled with tiny mollusks,
the air heavy as breath on the back of her neck.

A large body of water can hide so much—
farm houses and pasture and forests submerged

somewhere beneath the gray-green surface
of a lake, catfish big as train cars
in the cold, dark pocket below the dam. Secrets
tendered in driftwood and smooth stones.
Here, on the beach,
clouds seem to gather just beyond
the wind-lifted snarl of her hair.
But she is ready for weather that may blow in,
ready for gifts the tide will surely offer up.

We Had Been Promised
    July 3, 2003, *Go Deo* Robert

We had been promised: three days of rain
for every day without, so no surprise
to wake to that soft kind of gray, cloud-stain,
throat-thick. From separate beds, our eyes
followed rain splatter over window glass,
then outside, we convened, daring the storm
to interfere. That red Citron truck mud-splashed
our cuffs. A line of cows arced toward the barn
like a string of dusky pearls as we watched.
Your umbrella, you never opened it,
and soon the sunlight, golden-green, unlatched.
Inside our clasped hands, I felt your pulse tick—
hot coffee and the pages of books turning:
our rhythm, same as any other morning.

Our rhythm, same as any other morning,
in gentle pen-scratch on journal pages,
words which marked careful lives conjoining
as narrative. Ink of disparate ages
and geographies smeared into a new
shimmering language. Like braille, I waited
on the edge of the bed, thinking of you,
fingering skirt-spread satin. Lovely haint
hovering in the glass: woman I was,
or woman I would soon be? Laughter bold
in the doorway dissolved into young girls—
farm daughters bearing marsh marigold
and gray kittens. From warm fur and dress-shine,
rose that rumble which augured you always mine.

That rumble which augured you always mine:
deep in the creed I would only absorb
eight years later, but felt at that time,
distant and welcome, like the cool strum

of thunder on the hot roof of my heart.
It would unfurl as surely as a vine
in the morning sun, until my regret
was only in not receiving entwined
with you then. No matter, when the doors
of Dawros Church opened to evening sun
we drank in that light which sometimes pours
from Beara clouds, consecrated as one.
Smiling for photos, I felt my veil lift
and rise like fog clearing the bay, a gift.

Like fog clearing Kenmare Bay, a gift,
gilded voices floated up from a table
spread wide in an old schoolhouse attic.
Anchored by their stories, our lives able,
at last, to fix and shine as bright sea
creatures tide-safe in rocky Dingle pools.
Like rain-clouded water, my swirling litany
of steeping aggravations came loose.
Habits, yours and those of other boys—
really the whistling kettle of my own
self-doubt, which once steamed such garish noise—
vanished gently as wind-altered stone.
When a pub band played the Sex Pistols, we danced
close together, knowing nothing was chanced.

Close together, knowing nothing was chanced,
we drew away from the revelry—
hedgerows cast silver amid headlights' trance,
gravel-crunch beneath the tires when we
turned down the lane of that farmhouse inn.
You held my shoes and bouquet as I stepped
from the car. The next day, I would present
those flowers—an offering to tears wept
by an old woman in an empty teahouse.
But for now, you cradled them in your arms,
carefully as you later would both our infants.

Love's omen: that boy, slingshot drawn.
"See how far!" he cried, releasing the band.
Together, we watched rock rise never to land.

Together, we watched rock rise, nearing land
the next morning, as far below rushed
Dursey Sound. I held tight to your hand
until the creak of the cable car hushed,
leaving the two of us with my parents
to explore the cemetery where
amid purple loosestrife a black pony sent
pollen floating into sunlit air.
Atlantic winds had erased the print
from the cluster of ragged, gray stones,
but we gambled not pity lives spent
atop that cliff face—weather would hone
our own stories like those of times past
until they shined like sea-polished glass.

Your eyes shined bright as sea-polished glass
when, back on the mainland, alone once more
we drove through karst meadows, lost in the flash
of cracked limestone, each winter turlough's shore
remembered in dog violets crowning
a gryke. As the red sun hovered over
wild sea, all around us stone was browning,
warmed by evening light. I marked ground covered,
spreading our map and tracing the coast road
as we flew through the gloaming. Our landfall,
a Connemara room where we would
wake limb-tangled beneath rain's clear call
and stay in the warm sheets where we had lain,
grateful for that promise: three days of rain.

Still Life of Aunt Alice

In a photograph, my father's aunt holds fast to a sorrel gelding.
The grass is low and dry, windswept in September,
and the animal seems to have just shaken something off,
trace of quiver, fur stretched tight across hips and withers.
Her dress is calf length and plain, no tucks or pleats,
only the gentle curve of a cotton collar,
the shadows the breeze blows into the hem.
Woman and horse have come to an understanding.
The lead line is a wire, electric, between them,
but it is their eyes, wet and black, which secure the connection.
In that gaze, I, too, am animal, charmed,
following my own wrist, slender and blue-veined, back to where we start.

My father's stories cast other mysteries into relief—
that part of my grandfather lost before I even knew him,
lost to the South Pacific, to shrapnel blooming
indigo along the back of his thigh.
But what of the sister and horse anchored flat in old photography?
I've tried to sift her from that piece of bare pasture.
Years ago, I thought I felt her when I climbed the narrow staircase, and stepped across
sanded floor boards, light filtering through a tiny, round window, blue
slip of sky.
Too young to recognize family secrets, I felt my great aunt's ghost,
felt breath hovering just behind me, woman mad in the attic, there, suddenly,
gas hissing up from the stove top, a match that won't light.
Strange artifacts: these pieces they call handiwork—gentle
circles of crocheted lace, glass bottles painted
with the faces of blinking pansies—
and a photograph, which makes me crave something real.
The color of her voice, the sound of her gaze, how she talked to animals.

Gloria
December 31, 2013

Black-eyed peas are soaking,
but this year no ham-hock
waits nested in the frost-thick
interior of the muck room's deep freezer.
So little in this farmhouse
is as I remembered:
There is the rattle of pans without lids.
Ice thickens in the water trough,
and barn cats cry at the door.

For months she has subsisted
on cheeseburgers and bags of tacos
ordered off the bleary neon
of drive-through menus
while carefully spooning soft, comfort
food to her own mother
and reassurance
to my sisters and me.

My grandmother is two
days dead and I'm just realizing
how late I am, how much I've missed.
I'll have to drive to Food Lion,
where surely some old acquaintance
will shadow the butcher bin.

Next week, amid a scattering
of toddler toys and half-emptied
suitcases, Maeve will reach
again and again toward hollow air.
For days, my grandmother's given name
will bob like driftwood
on the foamy surface of her play.

For now, all I can do
is chop the collards, set
sausage sizzling in the pan.
Place a bowl on the table
tomorrow, place my baby girl
in my mother's lap tonight, hope
the two of them will be able
to fall asleep in this strange place.

My Own Skin

Even Stones Come to Rest: Julia Pastrana Considers Her Final Homecoming

I. Mother Tongue

In the camp of my girlhood
burros stomped and brayed
beneath a bower of ocotillo,

and dogs, half feral, tracked
the dust of expired fires.
Quite common: a child's bones

cracked by breech birth;
small limbs, shrunken further
with the scorpion's sting;
madness unleashed
from a poisoned tinaja.

Who would question this dark,
bearded child, *hija fea*? No one,
not once they watched me bend
firm over the yucca root
or walk long in the desert sun.

But who would hold tight to this hand
when offered such wealth?

II. Moonflower

The creamiest bloom
only at nightfall, so he came
to me in darkness. With the rough skin
split, every pitahaya reveals glistening fruit.

Gold throws humiliation into shadow,

and even my corsets were embroidered
with its shimmering threads.

An education:

in the unlacing. I sought
to absorb all I could,
knowing much
can rise up from the shaded,
lluvial plain—aware that

come monsoon season,
every cutbank washes away.

III. Moskva

I thought the child might
anchor me. For a moment,
snow feathering the glass
blurred beneath a narrow finger
of sunlight, transforming my cell
into a sparkling map of the entire world.

But when a late cold spell
froze carriage wheels to stone
and my gowns could no longer be
altered, our days begin to steep—
wood smoke and cabbage soup.

The chamber maid told me
that Russia feasts early,
and I dared imagine a bare crucifix
above my bed, labor's heat
pushing the arched branches of
Chestnuts into pale green bud.

How could I have known

that, cracked by fever,
we would both splinter
into pieces too small, too sharp,
to ever properly retrieve?

IV. Lirio

The prickly globe of cholla
is carried many miles
on the bristled haunch of the javelina,
and the bones of mice may desiccate
years before the spotted owl
pushes the pellet into hot sunlight,

but everything returns home.
Even stones
come to rest in the belly
of the canyon.
Dusted by lilies, my coffin shimmers
and waits. *Mi vida*, for a lock
of your dark hair, I would sacrifice
even this attempt at dignity.

The voice of the wind, pollen-scented,
will lull us all to sleep eventually—
this earth never stops
grinding itself into sand.

Space

The afternoon before Boyd begins Kindergarten
we lunch at a Japanese steakhouse.
I have prepared myself
as for a date, in his favorite blue dress,
in chandelier earrings, which, at his request,
I shake and jangle.

In the car, on the way here
he wanted to know—
How do planets stay in orbits?
Why is it so cold up there?
If a vacuum is nothing,
why can't something
just fill up that space?
Two weeks past his fifth birthday,
he's moved beyond questions
for which I have answers.

Here at the table, he shies briefly
before the flame, and I savor that shift,
the warm weight of his head against my torso,
the sound of his thumb sneaking
into his mouth. I try not to breathe,
knowing, as he doesn't, what is soon to be
unleashed: the juggling and flashing knives.
But already the *Shokunin* has bounced the first egg
off a blade, into his hat, and then back to the grill.

What was it my mother used to say
about not keeping them all in one basket?

Tomorrow, my son will stride
down the steps into the beginning
of his life without me. In truth,
summer has offered

one crosswalk after another
in which he failed to reach
for my hand, his own
universe ever-expanding.
But what did I do with my arms before
they sheltered him through intersections?

Somehow there is always comfort in food,
and the sizzling rice draws him back
to his own chair, but I feel—despite the warmth
the cook-top casts—that exact moment
the air conditioner clicks on in the ducts overhead
and the cold starts to settle between us.

Ordinary Time

8:00
Sud-splash,
double bath—
the soft edge
of a warm rag
between twenty toes,
neck scrub,
back rub
shark swim
soap scum,
bubbles off the nose.

8:30
Wet-drip—
watch your step—
tub slip
tile mop,
frog towels hung to dry.
Rug crawl
back sprawl
sugar bug
Toothbrush tug
as once again
he asks, why?

9:00
Pajamy-up.
Da scrapes sup,
mac-n-cheese
chiseled off
a plastic digger plate.
Lotioned limbs
And Laurie
Berkner hymns,
and, YES,

these are
the underwear
you said you hate.

9:30
Book-nook
bed shake,
once more
Who Made This Cake
—then lament
the mean porch light's gleam.
Blinds shut.
Noise cut.
Sheet shell, and
soft prayer until…
there—
the baby's sudden scream.

10:00
Open blouse—
cluttered house—
boob-soft
frantic suck—
Oh, fuck—
Am I completely dry?
Desperate wish
warm twist
milk moves,
and finally
something gentle
unwinds
inside our joint sigh.

10:30
Couch cove
touch toes
two friends
book-ends—

What's it going to be?
Find remote—
work note—
laugh track
heads back
we won't see the end
of Big Bang Theory.

11:00
Bed-dead
trash tread
dog pooped
laundry moved
sheets back
—Take care
she doesn't stir!
One last
email check—
try to soothe
student unrest—
then sink
—beneath ceiling fan's whir.

1:00
Red-faced
baby fright—
Hold tight!
legs kick
as if
she means
to crawl
back into my womb
warm sheets
milk-song,
limbs long
—Is she breathing?
Slow and deep,
nested sweet

in our bed's arcane tomb.

2:06, 3:47, 5:11?
Not sure
when the crying
finally stops
clock lags,
her weight sags
warm again.
Yet still, that hiccupy sob,
a constant warning.
So it's
gentle walk
and whisper-talk—
and sun slow
through kitchen window:
    a wafer
dissolving into morning.

Show-and-Tell, or Family Math

I forgot to include an item
in your backpack this morning—
something that starts with the letter "K"—
and you want to know why.

It wasn't that I failed
to read all eight parts of the kindergarten newsletter.
Neither was I confused by the six different fonts,
nor the unusual heading—those bold-face numbers
which, in fact, marked the dates of another week, long passed.
It might have been the two hours I sat
in my office on Sunday afternoon
while the three of you, minus me,
enjoyed the first weekend of fall—
September sunshine,
bluegrass strumming from the gazebo,
a funnel cake divided
beneath one of the two Black Walnut trees
remaining in Irvine McDowell Park.

It could have been
the mere four hours of sleep I average,
or, more specifically,
the way exhaustion multiplies
when that number is divided each time I rise
to nurse your eighteen-month-old sister
back to fitful slumber. But it just
as easily could have been
the six ounces of sugar-free chai,
which your father microwaved for two minutes,
and which I, lacking even five minutes
this morning, failed to drink.
Perhaps it was simply the continued
throbbing of the single toenail
I sacrificed to a car-shaped grocery cart

earlier in the week.
Even the smallest numbers add up.

More likely, it has something to do
with what I reasoned yesterday.
Upon returning from my 45 minutes at the YMCA,
I found the kitchen unbearably warm
amid the heat of your wet-faced sobbing.
And like deciphering a word problem,
I had to piece together the loss—
your sister, fallen from the second rung of the bunk bed,
now stood smiling, sucking a damp dishtowel,
but you, who had taunted her, cowered
your face into your father's chest
and clutched an ice pack to your forehead.

Da pushed me, you said,
and I lifted the compress
to find a bruise simmering like dusk
beneath the skin of your temple.
Meeting your father's eyes, I understood
the full weight of the equation.

Of course, I voiced incredulous anger:
You pushed our five-year-old child into a door frame?
But when I was alone, grading papers on the couch
as the sleep-sighs of all three of you
braided our living room's air tight around me,
I dared hold the plane of my own palm
beneath the lamp-light. How many times
had I felt the same urge flare like a struck match?
Then a current rushed back into my own chest—
the moon of your pale, shocked face
pulling at the ocean of my shame.

I rose and moved into the darkened space
beneath that same doorframe, and looked
into the room where you sprawled open-mouthed,

suddenly long-limbed and boy-tangled, in the sheets.
I couldn't say aloud how sorry I was,
and even if you had opened your eyes and sat up,
I couldn't have explained
what you were already learning
about the sheer scale of love's imperfection.

Fever-Cord

I have learned to trace illness through the damp
leaves of this forest, snuffle it hours
before it raises its pale head to stamp
the undergrowth of our quiet bowers,
inching up through the edge of her trusting
play, haunting us, a relentless shadow
companion. Her earth-damp breath rusting,
her eyes dimming like dusk-filled windows
in which I can track only my own worry.
Knowledge fails to prevent what will rise
sure as a rain-swollen wall of slurry—
I have learned not to pretend otherwise.

I will twist the hemp of my faith into a tether,
so that, just as before, we rise or sink together.

What Boyd Knows

When I get a new toy, you have to read the constructions.

When you shampoo my hair, I get watersick.

When I grow up, I will have mulch in my nose, just like you.

Before the community garden, this was all land.

Some days, I'm so special I have two shadows.

The stars are nocturnal, and so is the moon.

The Portuguese ocean is the same one from North Carolina.

No matter where we go, the moon follows.

My Own Skin

Last week, she swung
a bat into our television,
silencing Dora and leaving a crack
like the indigo web of some strange
spider etched across the inside
of a forever-dark flat screen.

When she wants
a princess Band-Aid,
she is not afraid to bite
her own hand hard
enough to taste blood.

Early this morning, after two
years of night nursing,
I turned off the baby monitor
and let her cry it out at 3 AM.
I woke to quiet sunshine,
but found she had removed her diaper
to pee through narrow crib slats—
not a drop on Eeyore or her ballerina PJs,
only a damp puddle
on the freshly-shampooed carpet.

My own mother loves to talk
of apples and the trees from which they fall.
At three, I poured a tub of glue
over the head of a boy who dared refuse
my kiss.

Maeve came into this world screaming,
and we blessed her with a secret
milk name in shocked whispers: *Tortuga*,
for the desperate stretch of her neck,
the snap of her gums against my nipple.

That first night, when colostrum failed
to satisfy, she wielded tight fists
and red-faced anger until I handed her
to a nurse who I knew would offer
a pacifier dipped in sugar water.

Now she has such a sweet tooth
that I hide my chocolate.

She is still young enough, our daughter,
to paint with her hands, spreading
an abstract scene over a long curl
of white butcher paper.
But some nights, when sleep bends her
like the sun-softened bloom of a daffodil,
the tail of her stuffed donkey becomes a brush,
and she paints my neck, my face.

On these nights,
when she goes down
easy, and I can settle
her soft as pollen into the crib,
I step across the hallway
and lean into the mirror
searching my own skin
for the story I know
she's left there.

Biohazard

I.
After weeks of cool rain, May blushes warm, but still
the Mountain laurel on the side of our house fails to bloom.
The leaves, dark and waxy beneath my fingertips, are rich
from the black soil—they have spread
as my daughter's placenta faded back into the earth
along with the slips of brightly colored paper
on which family and friends wrote blessings.

When we moved from Oklahoma,
I excavated an Indian laurel
and carried it across the country,
rattling the door of the van open
to pour cups of water over the root ball
which the same part of my first-born had nurtured.
Months later, that shrub, bred for hot summers,
froze on our deck, succumbing to the worst
ice storm in a dozen Kentucky winters.

After the thaw, I shook the soil from brittle roots
and let the pot rest, a quiet tabernacle,
in the shadow of the house. Come spring,
when neighbors divided lilies and left them
on our porch in a damp cardboard box,
we sprinkled a handful of the black dirt
before setting each plant into the ground.

II.
        A friend who grew up in rural Vietnam
claims his own mother hung his placenta
    before the nursery window
        where it dried slowly
           in the warmth of the rising sun.

      In Kenya, Kikuyu fathers swaddle the placenta
before burying it beneath an uncultivated field.
      Still other cultures burn it, collecting the ashes into a powder
          to be administered to the child in time of illness.

      Some believe it the infant's shadow spirit,
dark twin keeping the child safe on earth,
     then ushering the soul through death
        into the world which follows.

III.
      After thirty-eight hours of active labor,
I was so exhausted that I left behind my son's placenta.
My husband had to follow a labyrinth of corridors
deep into the bowels of the university hospital
to retrieve it, and he was suspicious of what
the nurse handed him—a plastic pan,
surprisingly heavy, my name etched
across the lid in permanent marker
next to the word *biohazard*.

     Three pounds lighter and positioned well,
my daughter shot into this world like a rocket—
I was still signing the hospital forms as she crowned,
so, of course, her placenta came home with us,
next to the suitcase we barely had time to open.

I held the placenta of the twins we never saw.
Weeks after the bleeding began, I let it go
in a public restroom.
I couldn't help but wonder:
        The well water I drank as a child?
        The chemical weapons being neutralized
          at the Bluegrass Army Depot just across town?

For our unborn, we planted Sweet Bay magnolias,
and as I watched the leaf blight spread,

I cursed myself yet again
for setting the trees too close
in that damp corner of the yard.

IV.
When my daughter had lived only weeks inside me,
I startled fledglings from a nest beneath the eaves.
Lifting the recycling bin, I hollered a greeting to a neighbor,
and the birds tumbled to the concrete, near-naked,
in a blur of bright beak and gray-tufted down.
The nest remained empty for two seasons.

Last May, when my baby girl, barely one,
spiked the first in a series of fevers,
each reddening her lips and prickling the fragile skin
of her rib cage, I wanted to become
the white eye-roll, the bird-limbed convulsions.
How I fret for the brood of robins returned this spring.

It is so hard not to track all the hurt the world might offer.
In December, after Sandy Hook, I blessed my son
with holy water before dropping him off at kindergarten.
Afternoons, if my daughter sleeps heavy,
I pass my palm before her parted lips
for the certainty of her soft exhalation.

But motherhood offers no easy assurance—
        I mourn for the black widows even as I burn
        their egg sacs from the corner of the sand box.